MIDLIFE CAREER COMBO

COMBINE YOUR PASSIONS. CREATE YOUR
LIFE'S WORK.

CASSANDRA GAISFORD

Blue
Giraffe

"Let the beauty you love be the work that you do."

~ Rumi

AUTHOR'S NOTE

As I write, it's the first of March 2021. Auckland, New Zealand's largest city has been hastily plunged into another lockdown. This time for a week. Two weeks ago, it was for three days. Who knows when we will next all be regulated and enforced to remain at home.

If there was ever a more immediate need to develop a Midlife Career Combo, it's now. Jobs, livelihoods, ways of working that have retained a modicum of feeling in our control are forever changed. Doors are shuttered, staff retrenched and lives disrupted.

As I share in this book, the only security you have nowadays are your saleable skills. Crisis and chaos can herald opportunity. When you combine your talents with inspiration and fill a need, you will find your joy and freedom.

INTRODUCTION

One of my coaching clients asked me this recently: "I keep asking myself how can I combine my love of travel, beautiful places and growth/learning with the skills of conceptualising, strategising, investigating, writing, and advising—while having time and location freedom and eventually earning an excellent living—as well as when starting out, allows me to maintain a full-time job and family? What's a stretch but still realistic?"

If you've been following me for a while now, you'll know I'm a big fan of the law of attraction and manifestation. Which I why I believe following what lights you up and speaks to your heart is a winning strategy. It also leaves plenty of room for what I call a Career Combo—a career that marries your passions, enthusiasms and soul purpose.

The truth is that a Midlife Career Combo will tick many boxes for you—including an aspect of learning and exploring things new to you. The fact is that any career change or business you start, even if a side-gig at first, will need a diverse skillset.

"Continue, as you are, to research the options and perhaps

put a ring around a date when you feel you will have done enough research and think it is time to make decisions," I shared with my client.

When I was investigating becoming <u>a career and life coach</u> I contacted people who offered life coaching as though I was a potential client and in some cases, I sat down with them to experience their process. And then I realised I didn't like the way they did things and I adapted and combined my diverse experiences to create my own unique way of working.

This is what I call, harnessing your PassionPoint—the intersection of your skills, talents, interests, purpose, values and goals etc. I talk more about this in my Midlife Career Rescue series of books. Gosh, I made such a great living when I focused on that and a great lifestyle too... Plus there was plenty of scope to diversify—thus feeding my love of variety.

The only security is your saleable skills

In today's unstable economic environment the only security is that you have a saleable skill. Not placing all your golden eggs in one industry or way of working allows you to hedge your bets and better ride the changing tides of fortune.

So it was super cool when my client emailed me back and told me that she had found a company that was working a 'Career Combo'. "I shared this with you as it confirms what you've been telling me all along, that you can combine passions," she wrote to me. And it inspired her to take a chance on her dreams.

My hope in writing this book is that you will be inspired too.

BOOK 1: THE CALL FOR A CAREER COMBO

WHAT IS A CAREER COMBO?

I invented this term many years ago, inspired by McDonald's BigMac Combos and other hamburger bundles. Essentially, it's a pick and mix approach to creating your career. Instead of fries with your current breadwinning career, you might add a side-hustle.

I did this when I was fed up with the politics and lack of freedom and the salary cap in my role as National Manager of Career Counselling for an EAP provider. I loved career counselling but I wanted to do things differently and I wanted to write books and I wanted to travel and not be stuck in a cubicle. So I started writing a column for the national newspaper, and I started my first company Worklife Solutions from the kitchen table and coached private clients during weekends.

Your Midlife Career Combo may have a very different kind of sauce. DJ Lemon, for example, is a barber by day. But a DJ by night.

If you've read my book, The Art of Success: Leonardo Da Vinci, or Coco Chanel, you'll know that artists can teach all of us, no matter what your career trajectory so much about passion, perseverance and variety. Currently, my Midlife

Career Combo includes writing romance novels as Mollie Mathews; creating healing art and writing self-empowerment books as Cassandra Gaisford. Plus I am a life and career coach and I train other passionate purposeful people who would love a lifestyle career to become Certified Worklife Solutions Coaches too.

These careers are all sandwiched between my love of empowering others, creating and sharing beauty, healing, hope and joy—and sending more love into the world, amongst other things.

I share more examples of Midlife Career Combos in the pages that follow. You'll also find plenty to inspire you in Midlife Career Rescue. Or, as many of my clients have, after reading the book, you'll come to me for individual guidance, encouragement and support

Remember, success is defined by the things you say yes to—and by taking a chance on your dreams.

WHY DO A CAREER COMBO?

There are as many reasons as there are variations. Increased satisfaction, flexibility of lifestyle, diversity of income, reducing the frustration of a boring or stressful job with one that brings joy and pleasure. Increased freedom, planning or trialling a new career. Balancing other roles—wife, mother, a caregiver—with childcare or other needs and demands. Or a need to reduce mounting debts.

Then there is the creative mind, like mine, which needs diversity to thrive, and roles that are divined. In Pam Gregory's wonderful book, *How to Co-create Using the Secret Language of the Universe: Using Astrology For Your Empowerment* I am advised that I am a born multi-tasker and am destined to have two careers (or more) running simultaneously at once.

How about you? Why could a Midlife Career Combo work for you?

WHO CAN DO A CAREER COMBO?

A nyone can combine careers to create a rewarding life. Retirees, dissatisfied employees or business owners, or those planning their next inspired career move. A Midlife Career Combo is perfect for creatives who bore easily and thrive on diversity.

A Midlife Career Combo is perfect for mum's considering returning to work or wanting to earn an income on the side. Or people who want to balance a lucrative career they hate with something on the side that fills them with pride. The truth is, anyone can do a Career Combo.

Who do you know who has a Midlife Career Combo?

4

WHERE CAN YOU DO A CAREER COMBO?

You can work your Midlife Career Combo in a variety of locations. It may be while sipping cocktails lying in a hammock overlooking the sea. Your Midlife Career Combo may sprout by planting herbs in an underused portion of the garden. Or by turning a neglected garage into a beautiful art gallery.

Your Midlife Career Combo may germinate at the local farmers' markets, in a portable food truck or in a pop-up-store. You may not even have to leave the comfort of your pyjamas or the tranquillity of your home.

So many people say "I can't do this and I can't do that because of Covid" or some other excuse. You can do your Midlife Career Combo from anywhere with a little bit of creative thinking and know-how.

It's time to get your thinking hat on!

WHAT HAPPENS WHEN YOU NEGLECT THE CALL FOR A CAREER COMBO?

W hen you neglect the call to change your career and life unpleasant side effects can include:

- Stagnation and lack of growth
- Boredom and depression
- Frustration and fatigue
- Increased stress
- Poor mental, emotional, physical, and spiritual health
- Relationship strain
- Inability to adapt to changing economic circumstances
- Feeling stuck in a rut
- Regret, knowing you could be doing something more interesting
- And a whole swag of other things

BOOK 2: DISCOVER YOUR CAREER COMBO

BE OBSESSED

F ollowing your obsessions is a wonderful way to get in the zone of discovering something different, improving your workday and transforming your life. What fascinates you? It could be anything:

- Astrology
- Beekeeping
- Cooking
- Yoga
- Zoo keeping

Or something else? Troll through the alphabet or ask a friend for ideas about your obsessions. Consider combining a loud obsession with a quiet obsession, or something in completely the opposite direction.

DJ Lemon loves vinyl records and the noise of parties. By day he loves the quietness of cutting men's hair. Dave Crabb loves to skate. His combo includes building houses and designing skateboard ramps.

Care for your heart and do what makes you spark.

YOU WANT WHAT?!#@

I t's not where you are it's how and who and where you want to be. Spending time figuring out what you need to feel totally on fire is a smart Career Combo strategy.

Where's your happy place? Do you need the constant buzz of people around you? Or would all those interactions drive you nuts? Do you love to travel? Or is seclusion your go-to strategy?

Different Midlife Career Combos have different requirements, just as you have different needs to feel happy, productive and satisfied. Before jumping into decision making make sure you get clear about what lights you up.

CLUES TO YOUR COMBO

How will you know if your Midlife Career Combo is right for you? One of the most reliable measures is your heart. Some common signs include your passions and what lights you up:

- A burning desire or hunger
- A feeling of inspiration
- A feeling in the pit of the stomach
- A sense of excitement
- A state of arousal
- A feeling of limitless energy
- A clarity of vision
- A feeling that nothing is too much trouble
- A sense of caring deeply
- A feeling of contentment

KEEP A CAREER COMBO JOURNAL

This is where manifesting your preferred future really happens. I've been keeping various manifestation journals for years and so many things I've visualised and affirmed on the pages, are now my living realities.

Keep track of the times you notice clues to your passion, purpose, and Midlife Career Combo potential. Record these insights in an inspirational journal so that they don't get lost or forgotten.

Adding quotes, articles, pictures, and insights from this book. Taking stock of anything that reinforces the things that make you leap for joy will really make your journal come alive.

Gain greater awareness of what is driving your Midlife Career Combo by asking yourself, "Why am I passionate about this? Why does this look or feel like a good option for me?"

Look for the themes and patterns that build up over time. Keep feeding your belief by referring to your Midlife Career Combo journal regularly and looking for more ways to add passion to your life.

VISUALIZE YOUR PREFERRED FUTURE

D id you know you are living the life you have consciously or subconsciously visualised? See your way to success.

Try to visualise your preferred future by closing your eyes and imagining a time in the future 1, 5, or 10 years from now. What are you doing? Who is there? How are you feeling? Walk toward the future and look back to today. What steps did you take to get there?

If you spend time imagining the future you want, you have without even knowing it begun to make it happen.

VOCATIONS & VACATIONS

W hat you do for a living plays a major role in your happiness and wellbeing. When you do what you love, work doesn't feel like a chore at all. If you plan it well, your chosen vocation can feel like a vacation and wash away the dust of everyday life.

As I shared in *Midlife Career Rescue*, I found my Midlife Career Combo after listening to song lyrics! "I dream I'm on vacation, it's the perfect career for me," sang the Eagles.

Work is not WORK It is not a job. I don't have to grit my teeth and go to my cubicle and bear it. It's who I am and what I do. I am called to serve through my passion and purpose and in doing so I am following my bliss.

"It seems to me that A Midlife Career Combo is what you do. You're a business owner of a counselling service, a counsellor, a career coach, and a student... did I miss anything?" I asked one of my clients recently.

"I think you have all of the things I am in my professional life, yet **I feel it is all of my life** (bold added by me). So is that a vocation?" she replied.

If you have a vocation, you have a strong feeling that you

are doing the work you were born to do. You will feel especially suited to do it, and you will feel you are fulfilling a particular role in life, especially one which involves helping other people.

One of the reasons I write my self-empowerment books and create healing, uplifting art is to bring more peace, joy and beauty into peoples lives. Peace is my WHY. Peace is my PASSION. Peace is how I SERVE. And these are roles which I know in my soul I am well suited to.

How can you find your vocation? What song lyrics, poetry or aspirational quotes might illuminate your path?

OPPOSITES ATTRACT

People often think a career has to be just one thing. You have to work in either health or art and can't marry two seemingly opposite careers.

Men and women marry their opposites all the time, right? The differences, rather than be oppositional in a bad way, make the vibrational pull stronger.

Make integrating your obsessions your next obsession. Figure out a way to combine completely opposite careers. Ask open-ended questions and seek input from others.

Let your intuition do the talking. Ask, "How can I combine art and health?" Put it out to the Universe—or Facebook as I recently saw one jobseeker do. Art therapist, rehabilitation nurse, artist and gallery owner (me) are some possible Career Combos that mingle art and health that immediately come to be mind.

Push through. Go beyond the obvious. Asking, "what? why, how, where?" may yield interesting results. Look for examples of others who have a happy and successful career marriage.

Wait for your eureka moment when your heart jumps with joy, and sings, "Yes, that's what I want to do."

BOOK 3: CAREER COMBO AT WORK

CRAZY EGG

Pursuing several careers at once might seem crazy, but not only is it a growing trend, for some—especially as they start out— it's the only way to earn money doing what they love.

James Patterson kept his day job as a lawyer and penned crime novels on the side. He now writes in a variety of genres and has mastered the art of writing short, impactful books which satisfy his voracious readers.

Author C.J. Lyons continued to work as a paramedic while building her career writing thrillers. She said it took seven books before she started to see a regular income stream.

Mary Bly enjoys her salaried position as a tenured professor of English Literature while penning Regency and Georgian romance novels under her pen name, Eloisa James.

How can you follow your passion and still pay the bills?

You'll find more suggestions in the chapters which follow and also my book *Mid-Life Career Rescue: Employ Yourself.*

WHAT'S YOUR GIG?

The latest way of working, a friend told me recently, is doing gigs. While it's not that new the term maybe. As is employers readiness to ditch permanent employees.

The Gig Economy is a rapidly developing labour market defined by short-term contracts or freelance work. Permanent jobs may soon be like Tyrannosaurs—a relic of the past. In a Gig Economy, you are paid for the "gigs" you do, such as food delivery, a car journey, a short-term contract and a whole host of other things.

My 2021 foray into writing for New Zealand House and Garden fits the definition of a gig. I was contracted and paid to write a specific piece, with a specific number of words, for a specific price.

A gig doesn't provide much certainty, but I like the flexibility and freedom of gigs. I have to balance that joy with the uncertainty of income and future work. This is why a Midlife Career Combo is perfect.

Defining and refining your own Midlife Career Combo will help you pay the mortgage—assuming you have created multiple income streams. It will help you feel in control and minimise feelings of angst or being exploited. Plus you'll get ahead of the wave. The only security you have in these uncertain times is that you have saleable skills—ideally in areas you enjoy.

How could you find fulfilling work as a short-term, temporary, or independent contractor for one or a variety of employers, clients or customers?

MULTI-TALENTED

P eople may have told you you have a range of skills or perhaps you have discovered this for yourself.

Your favourite knacks and natural talents, as well as those skills you have developed, is a perfect place to forage for your Midlife Career Combo.

Writing, painting, selling, designing furniture, interior design, graphic design, healing, massage . . .the possibilities are endless. Combine your skills with your interests to broaden your awareness of possible Midlife Career Combos you feel you would enjoy.

Skills are like stars, they cluster around who you are. They shine brightest when you follow what lights you up and who you want to be.

If the Universe gave you a writing skill, it will support you in everything—you may have to work at it, but you were given that talent. Beyoncé wasn't given her voice so she could sit on her butt and be a typist.

Kamala Harris wasn't given her compassion and fierce intellect to hide under a bushel and stay quiet. Show up, engage your talents, collaborate with a like-minded community, and dazzle the world with your amazing brilliance.

Leonardo da Vinci wasn't blessed with a curious mind and exquisite artistic talents so he could follow in his father's shoes and be an actuary. Nor, did he subscribe to Julia Cameron's, author of *The Artist's Way*, statement: "If you are good at more than one thing you get punished for it." Leonardo was a polymath—he wasn't born to be nor do one thing.

Where are your points of brilliance? How have you been blessed with natural gifts? How can you shine and make your life more dazzling? Who could you combine talents with to become legendary?

HAPPY HOBBIES

Happy hobbies can reveal hidden Midlife Career Combo options. You may not want to monetise your passion but many people do. There's a reason people say "when you do what you love you never work again." That's because it's true.

When you do what you enjoy getting paid for it is an extra special treat. Jenny loves baking and has turned it into a rewarding career, blending it with another love—teaching, she's never been happier.

As a child, Max loved collecting exotic butterflies. Now in his 60s, he combines a stressful financial career as a mortgage expert with sourcing specimens for collectors around the world.

What makes you happy? How could your hobbies transform your work and life?

PLAY WITH MATCHES

Sometimes, while discovering your perfect Midlife Career Combo you need to play with different interests and activities to find the thing that really ignites the spark.

Give yourself permission to try new things and to follow the things that light a fire in your soul.

Give up the need to be good or excellent or for them to have any value in the short-term. Don't concern yourself initially with whether they will pay the bills. Hang onto your bread and margarine job a bit longer to create some space and freedom from worrying about how the bills will get paid.

As Hollywood screenwriting guru, Aaron Sorkin shares, "Go ahead and take chances because that's the only way you're actually gonna find out where your sweet spot is."

Light up the world by following what lights you up. Your sweet spot will be completely unique from what lights me up. There are no wrong paths, no whopping mistakes, no fail-proof step-by-step life plan etched into granite by the big G.

Play around and take chances by diving into new experiences and testing longings. Experiment and see if the desire to integrate what lights you up into your Midlife Career Combo grows stronger.

FOLLOW THE CURVEBALLS

Very often, it's not until life throws us a curveball that we go in search of answers. When I was embarking on a career change, stressed out of my mind, suffering shingles, I devoured every book and every strategy which could help me not only survive but thrive. I share many of these tools in my books, including: *Stress Less,* Mid-Life Career Rescue and *Bounce: Overcoming Adversity, Building Resilience and Finding Joy*

The chaotic curveballs life was throwing at me led to a new career as a career counsellor. I later redesigned this one-thing career into a Midlife Career Combo as an entrepreneur, author, columnist, and teacher. Amongst plenty of other things. Later still, I added being an artist and gallery owner to my Midlife Career Combo by shedding some things and adding others.

What curveballs is life throwing at you? What is life urging you to do or become? For a super-duper inspirational talk on how trauma led to purpose, check out super-talented actress Viola Davis revealing how she rose beyond her tragic childhood>> https://youtu.be/5QWsfnp2LaU

19

BOUNCEY WORK

I f Monday mornings are a low point in your week, it may be a sign that it's time for a new career. And you're not alone. Research shows that less than 10% of people are visibly working with passion and purpose.

Career dissatisfaction, aching boredom, and gnawing unfulfillment are common causes of stress, low productivity, poor performance and plummeting levels of confidence and self-esteem.

To find a job you truly love an easy place to start is to use current things getting you down as signposts to your preferred future. Confirming what's causing your job blues will put more bounce into your career and help you get clear about your intentions, options, and possibilities.

Another great strategy is spending more time getting to know you, getting clear about who you are and what you need to feel happy and fulfilled. You'll then be better able to bounce toward a new career.

What are your bounce factors? What makes you jump for joy? If you want to feel happy in your job you need to be clear about all the things that make you feel passionate and alive.

Some things to consider include:

• Your core values, beliefs, and deepest interests
• Your strengths, gifts, and talents, you love doing
• The sort of work environment that best suits you
• What sort of people you want to work with
• Your personality and what makes you tick
• The things that give your life meaning and purpose
• What you love!

"There is no mistaking love. You feel it in your heart. It is the common fibre of life, the flame that heals our soul, energises our spirit and supplies passion to our lives," says psychiatrist, Elizabeth Kubler-Ross. Don't give up until you've found the things that ignite your soul.

You'll find plenty of inspiration and practical strategies in my *Mid-life Career Rescue series*, and *How to Find Your Passion and Purpose* and also my online course *Follow Your Passion to Prosperity.*

20

BE WHO YOU ARE'S

D id you know that you have a variety of personalities? What's more, have multiple voices is normal—not mad, bad or sad. A counselling approach called Family Systems therapy recognises that we all have multiple facets of our personality.

One member of our personality family may be noisy; one facet may be quiet; one facet may be reckless; the other studious. Another still may be naughty—the other sweet and cute and so, so, so nice.

Harness the power of these different personalities to unleash and define your Career Combo and add some spice. For example, Laurie is a former bank manager. One of his personalities is that he is cautious and financially prudent. But another Laurie is pioneering and thrives on taking extreme risks.

A Midlife Career Combo allows his personalities to come out to play on different days and in different ways. He regularly takes time out of his serious and stressful career as a mortgage expert to research rare butterflies in the jungles of Papua New Guinea.

Perhaps, you recognise the "inner critic' aspect of your personality. Then there is that annoying member of your personality that is always, so, so, so negative. "You can't do that!" "You'll never succeed." "You'll never make any money." In the final section of this book, you'll find plenty of helpful ways to prevent the critic from steering you away from your path with heart.

21

DON'T CHASE THE MARKET

"How do you make a living from your Midlife Career Combo?" I hear you ask. Spot a gap, create a need, or fulfil anticipated needs and desires. Don't chase the market. Chances are there's plenty of people already fishing in that pond.

For example, when I created my art gallery, Art@Rangitane, the Kerikeri housing market was booming. More and more new homes were being built. More homes meant more white walls. And guess what? There wasn't an art gallery in sight. The only thing that existed was a tiny gift shop. People were looking for large paintings and art customised to suit their new homes. Art that was uplifting, beautiful and inspiring.

Spot and create a niche. Don't be deterred if at first you don't succeed. Do what you dream about and wait for the world to catch up. No one really knows what, or who will be the next hot thing.

Persevere with your vision. Let the beauty you love be the work that you do. Cocoon yourself in the protective magic and power of creative, lateral, blue-skies thinking.

Looking for a job? You'll helpful tips in Mid-Life Career Rescue Job Search Strategies That Work.

22

REAL RESILIENCE

The collapse of celebrity chef Jo Seagar's company in the wake of the 2010 Christchurch earthquakes didn't sink her but forced a rethink.

What could she control? She couldn't stop the earth from shaking, but she could keep hearts soaring.

Her new Midlife Career Combo includes writing columns about delicious food, cooking, and taking groups of women on food, photography and travel tours. While Covid-19 brought international travel to a screeching halt, she bounced with aplomb into the domestic market.

Jo's also passionate about her voluntary role as Patron and ambassador of Hospice NZ and mingles fundraising with cooking classes. Stay tuned for news of a new edition to her Midlife Career Combo—writing fiction with themes of finding love again after loss.

"It's actually the story of my life...I'm often retraining and moving across career paths....nursing to epidemiology research to cooking to restaurant running...catering company…food styling for commercials and cookbook production—my own 20 or so cookbooks.

Cafes, writing columns, television cooking shows… magazines, more cafe consultancy…cook school…retail kitchenware, hotel accommodation provider…tour leader overseas…modelling contract with L'Oréal. Then there are local foodie photography tours with bigger ones planned— the old Silk Road; Antarctica; rural japan and the fiords of Norway on the plans as soon as the borders open.

The constant has been my work for hospice for about 25 years now. My role as ambassador and Patron is to raise funds and public awareness of their work. My cooking classes are for their benefit too. I'm always wearing my hospice hat—or rather an apron."

Putting your passion and purpose centre stage not only helps you to whip up the ultimate Midlife Career Combo but also helps boost your resilience after setbacks.

23

STAY REGULAR

When are you Career Combo-ing? During weekends? Nights? Or sandwiching your passions in between your regular job and busy life?

You may be hoping your Career Combo or side hustle may be your next big thing, but history shows breakthroughs take time to climb.

Pick a time when your energy and motivation and ability to focus are at their peak. For me, mornings and evenings are my prime times. Other times batching my combo works just fine. Mondays and Tuesdays for writing. Wednesdays and Thursdays for coaching and Fridays for admin and other things. Weekends for playing with paint.

Of course, I'm free to break these rules. Because I'm self-employed I get to choose. Whatever you decide, stay regular so you can hit your stride.

BOOK 4: LIVE YOUR COMBO!

24

LIVE WITH PASSION AND PURPOSE

Doing work that is your passion and purpose is the ideal. However, if it isn't possible to create a Midlife Career Combo at this time then try to find other outlets for the things that light you up. Add something to your life that you are passionate about. It could be a hobby, sport or volunteer work.

What groups or organisations could you join to experience more of the things you are passionate about? Are there any opportunities in your community or among your friends?

Sometimes, gifting your time or volunteering in some capacity can open doors that would have otherwise remained shut. Be of service and the world may serve you too.

25

STAYING SANE

A year of Covid has challenged all of us. Who knows when or if the upheavals will end. As I write this chapter there appears to be no end in sight. So staying sane seems an even stronger message.

The following email from a former coaching client prompted me to add this chapter.

"I suspect I'll be on hold with my travel business for the remainder of the year. Who knew we'd still be dealing with Covid! Also, I'm not going to lie, managing work, family, coach training, and now even Spanish 😊, is a lot. But I'm energized and a good part of that is thanks to your coaching."

My sanity juice includes massages, meditation, affirmations, maintaining boundaries—and importantly, following my purpose and doing what I love.

What or who can help keep you sane and energised?

26

DOUBTS AND DREAMS

Doubts are like rancid meat. They poison everything upon which you'd love to feast. It's not about ignoring them, it's about choosing healthier thoughts for your I-can-do-it-diet. Inspect, analyse, question. Are your fearful thoughts true? Could you choose to accept that the doubt exists and try to handle it? Or are you best to chuck your doubts in the waste-of-energy bin?

Your doubts are your traitors. Your dreams are your saviours. How can you turn your doubts and fears into fuel for brilliance? Helen Frankenthaler faced a barrage of obstacles as a woman desiring to become a successful artist during the 1950s. She confessed privately to having a sad view of life and struggling in the valley between doubt and dreams. But the face she presented to the world was one of strong will, huge ambition and fortified self-belief. She set about burying her melancholy in manic activity—creating beautiful and original art.

Be your biggest fan. Back yourself 100%. We all have doubts, but it's amazing how your doubts will disappear once you are doing the things you love.

27

FEAR NOT FAILURE

D o you spend more time thinking of ways you could fail rather than ways you could succeed?

So often we don't give ourselves permission to make mistakes or to learn. Don't worry about failure. It's seldom fatal. Worry about the chances you miss when you're too afraid to try.

When was the last time you tested your fears? Look for and collect examples of people who have turned "failure" into success. To get started, revisit Jo Seagar's story in the chapter Real Resilience. What matters most is bouncing back after setbacks. You can. And you will.

28

NASTY OR NICE

If you are steering towards having more joy, fun and passion in your career and life, people may be jealous or threatened and criticise you. Do your Midlife Career Combo anyway!

Don't be put off by negative feedback. Don't wait for others to give approval to your life. Send your critics packing.

Be brave. Be bold. Be firm. Be audacious. You'll soon conquer your fears and convince others.

Who could you look to for inspiration, encouragement, and support? Keep away from people who throw ice on your ambitions. Small-minded people always do that, but the really brilliant minds make you feel that you, too, can become brilliant.

Check out the first book in my Transformational Super Kids series, *The Little Princess*, to learn how I sent my critics away!

29

SHIFT INGRAINED BELIEFS

"You've got to believe in what you're doing. You can't stay in the void of self-doubt. It's holding you back. It's like a bike—you've got to let go of the training wheels and say, "I can do this. I can do this without the training wheels.""

Does the quote above say something to you? It did to me. That was my partner giving me a motivational blast, back in March (2015).

My previous lack of confidence surprised so many people who knew me. I've always adopted the 'fake it 'till you make it' policy when needed. But self-doubt had always held me back from tackling some of the bigger projects I yearned to do.

I've been reasonably confident at things I didn't enjoy as much, or where there seemed to be less at stake. But I've been less believing when it came to following passions that seemed so beyond my capability.

"You can't make a living from something you love," a

woman told one of my coaches, recently. I hear that all the time. You might have too. Or, maybe deep down, there's a persistent voice telling you, you're not good enough, or you can't have what you want.

But what if the opposite were true? What if making a living from what you love is exactly what you can do.

It's the messages you tell yourself that matter most, says celebrity Hypnotherapist and Author Marisa Peers. "Belief without talent will get you further than talent with no belief. If you have the two you will be unstoppable."

Chances are you don't need to see a therapist to move beyond self-limiting beliefs, but if you do, great. Go do it. There's magic in that.

30

DAILY TONIC

F illing your own needs is not something that you do randomly, it's something that needs to be done on a regular basis. Make your passion and purpose a regular event. How consistently do you spend time doing things you enjoy? Can you do something every day to help keep your passion alive?

Only 15 or 30 minutes a day devoted to activities you love, and to those that move you closer to your dreams, can make a big difference to your health and happiness.

If finding the time or lacking energy is preventing you from doing more of the things you are passionate about, develop a strategy to restore the balance.

31

OVERCOME OBSTACLES

As Basketball superstar, Michael Jordan, once shared, "Obstacles don't have to stop you: If you run into a wall, don't turn around and give up. Figure out how to climb it, go through it, or work around it."

The reality is that anything worth having usually means conquering a few challenges along the way.

Obstacles don't have to stop you but they do require you to persevere in the face of setbacks. Sometimes all you need is a few different ways of getting around whatever stands before you and your goals.

There is never a setback that doesn't create an opportunity. But many people give up at the first hurdle. They say things like, "It's hard to find the time," or "I don't have any skills," or "It's a tough economy." How do you look at things? Do you look at all the obstacles or do you proactively seek opportunities?

While circumstances may hamper your progress they don't have to stop you. Get into the habit of viewing any obstacles as challenges—ones which when overcome will boost your self-esteem and confidence and provide you with additional skills to tackle your dreams with added zest. This attitude shift will help you approach setbacks with the all-important ingredient—a positive state of mind.

Study the list below. How many of these words are part of your everyday chatter? Say them out loud now and tune into how they make you feel. Do they make you feel strong, confident and resourceful? Or do they make you feel stuck, depressed and anxious?

Affirm what you want by actively replacing these and any other disempowering words you currently use with powerful words and questions that boost your confidence and help you to identify solutions to any possible challenges you may be experiencing.

Disempowering Words

- I can't
- It's hard
- Problem
- By myself
- Setback
- I'm budgeting
- I can't afford it
- I will never be able to do it
- I should
- I'm a failure. I'll never get it right.
- I'm scared
- What other disempowering words come to mind?

Empowering Words

- I can; How can I? I'll find a way

- It's a challenge
- Challenge
- With myself
- Learning experience/opportunity
- I'm saving
- How can I afford it?
- How can I find a way? I'll find a way
- I choose
- What have I learnt? I'll get it right next time
- I'm stretching my comfort zone
- What other empowering words come to mind?

Smart people focus on their biggest rock. What's the biggest obstacle blocking your quest for self-employed success? How can you swarm all over it and give it all of your effort until it no longer poses a threat?

PERSISTENT DESIRE

T hings worth having in life don't always come easily. You have to want something with such a passion that you're willing to persevere in the face of setbacks. Every time you persist in the face of setbacks your belief in yourself will skyrocket until it reaches the point where you become unstoppable!

How persistent are you? Do you give up easily? How can you keep yourself motivated to put in the time and energy it may take to move ahead and reach your goals?

Daily Action

One of the most effective ways to tackle any obstacles is daily action—even if it consists only of baby steps. Just 15 minutes a day devoted to activities that move you in the direction of your dreams can make a major difference. A phone call, an email, a chat with a friend over coffee, some research or reading helpful material will help maintain a posi- tive, 'can do' mindset.

By focusing your energy and time on your preferred

future you will tap into the amazing power of the Law of Attraction by keeping your energy levels high. So high that with time and effort you will rise above any obstacles in your path.

Maintain faith and a positive expectancy that your dreams are manifesting. Maintaining a strong belief, coupled with positive action, is the foundation to creating your heart's desires. Every day positively affirm that you have already achieved or exceeded your dream. Act 'as if' and challenge reality to catch up.

The seeds that you have planted are beginning to sprout. You may not even be aware of these results however since they are in their infancy. Now it is more important than ever to stay positive and fertilise your seeds of creation with the right nutrients. These include a strong, positive vision of your preferred future, a positive expectancy, a commitment to solutions and affirming thoughts.

As his Holiness The Dalai Lama wisely once said, "Positive thoughts are like flowers, they need watering every day."

GRAB YOUR FREE GIFT!

The Passion Journal: The Effortless Path to Manifesting Your Love, Life, and Career Goals

Thank you for your interest in my new book.
To show my appreciation, I'm excited to be giving you another book for FREE!

Download the free *Passion Journal Workbook* here>>https://dl.bookfunnel.com/aepj97k2n1

I hope you enjoy it—it's dedicated to helping you live and work with passion, resilience and joy.

You'll also be subscribed to my newsletter and receive free giveaways, insights into my writing life, new release advance alerts and inspirational tips to help you live and work with passion, joy, and prosperity. Opt-out at any time.

ALSO BY CASSANDRA GAISFORD

Transformational Super Kids:

The Little Princess
The Little Princess Can Fly
I Have to Grow
The Boy Who Cried
Jojo Lost Her Confidence
Lulu is a Black Sheep
Why Doesn't Mummy Love Me?

Mid-Life Career Rescue:

The Call for Change
What Makes You Happy
Employ Yourself
Job Search Strategies That Work
3 Book Box Set: The Call for Change, What Makes You Happy, Employ Yourself
4 Book Box Set: The Call for Change, What Makes You Happy, Employ Yourself, Job Search Strategies That Work

Career Change:

*Think Outside The Box: How to Change Careers with
Creative Thinking*

Career Change 2020 5 Book-Bundle Box Set

Master Life Coach:

Leonardo da Vinci: Life Coach

Coco Chanel: Life Coach

The Art of Living:

How to Find Your Passion and Purpose

*How to Find Your Passion and Purpose Companion
Workbook*

*Career Rescue: The Art and Science of Reinventing Your
Career and Life*

Boost Your Self-Esteem and Confidence

Anxiety Rescue

No! Why 'No' is the New 'Yes'

How to Find Your Joy and Purpose

How to Find Your Joy and Purpose Companion Workbook

The Art of Success:

Leonardo da Vinci

Coco Chanel

Journaling Prompts Series:

The Passion Journal

The Passion-Driven Business Planning Journal

How to Find Your Passion and Purpose 2 Book-Bundle Box Set

Health & Happiness:

The Happy, Healthy Artist
Stress Less. Love Life More
Bounce: Overcoming Adversity, Building Resilience and Finding Joy
Bounce Companion Workbook

Mindful Sobriety:

Mind Your Drink: The Surprising Joy of Sobriety
Mind Over Mojitos: How Moderating Your Drinking Can Change Your Life: Easy Recipes for Happier Hours & a Joy-Filled Life
Your Beautiful Brain: Control Alcohol and Love Life More

Happy Sobriety:

Happy Sobriety: Non-Alcoholic Guilt-Free Drinks You'll Love
The Sobriety Journal
Happy Sobriety Two Book Bundle-Box Set: Alcohol and Guilt-Free Drinks You'll Love & *The Sobriety Journal*

Money Manifestation:

Financial Rescue: The Total Money Makeover: Create Wealth, Reduce Debt & Gain Freedom

The Prosperous Author:

Developing a Millionaire Mindset
Productivity Hacks: Do Less & Make More
Two Book Bundle-Box Set (Books 1-2)

Creativity:

Play Dates: Insights and Inspiration to Spark and Sustain Your Creativity

Miracle Mindset:

Change Your Mindset: Millionaire Mindset Makeover: The Power of Purpose, Passion, & Perseverance

Non-Fiction:

Where is Salvator Mundi?

More of Cassandra's practical and inspiring workbooks on a range of career and life-enhancing topics are on her website (www.cassandragaisford.com) and her author page at all good online bookstores.

NOW IN AUDIO!

Did you know you can enjoy and be inspired by Cassandra's most popular and successful books on audio? In less than 15 minutes you could be listening your way to a new life!

Check out the following written and narrated by Cassandra:

**Mid-Life Career Rescue: The Career For Change
How to Find Your Passion and Purpose**

How to Find Your Joy and Purpose
The Little Princess
The Little Princess Can Fly
I Have to Grow
The Boy Who Cried

Audio versions of these and other titles available now from all online bookstores and libraries.

NEW RELEASES COMING SOON

Word By Word:Lessons on Writing, Love, and Life

ABOUT THE AUTHOR

Cassandra Gaisford, is a holistic therapist, award-winning artist, and #1 bestselling author. A corporate escapee, she now lives and works from her idyllic lifestyle property overlooking the Bay of Islands in New Zealand.

She is called 'the queen of uplifting inspiration' and is best known for the passionate call to redefine what it means to be successful in today's world.

Cassandra is a well-known expert in the area of success, passion, purpose and transformational business, career and life change, and is regularly sought after as a keynote speaker, and by media seeking an expert opinion on career and personal development issues.

Cassandra has also contributed to international publications and been interviewed on national radio and television in New Zealand and America.

She has a proven track record of successfully helping people find savvy ways to boost their finances, change careers, build a business or become a solopreneur—on a shoestring.

Cassandra's unique blend of business experience and qualifications (BCA, Dip Psych.), creative skills, and wellness and holistic training (Dip Counselling, Reiki Master Teacher) blends pragmatism and commercial savvy with rare and unique insight and out-of-the-box-thinking for anyone wanting to achieve an extraordinary life.

WORK WITH ME

"Women are always told, 'You're not going to make it, it's too difficult, you can't do that, don't enter this competition, you'll never win it.' They need confidence in themselves and people around them to help them to get on."

~ Dame Zaha Mohammad Hadid, architect

Work with me! Get your mojo back. Reach out to me for spiritual guidance, career coaching, <u>training</u> and more. Take a chance!

While I am an advocate for alternative approaches to coaching and healing, I also value evidence-based techniques. My evidence is gained both from the extensive work I have done with clients, and also the transformational change I have created in my own life including:

- Leaving a job I hated and creating one I love
- Finding a loving relationship after years of loneliness
- Raising a daughter as a single parent
- Overcoming social anxiety and my fear of public

speaking and presenting my passion-driven work model to a global audience

- Bouncing back from suicidal ideation following a failed engagement
- Supporting loved ones through periods of extreme despair, including substance abuse, relationship abuse and attempted suicides
- Releasing my fear of judgment, standing out from the crowd and fear of failure
- Breaking free of self-sabotaging behaviour— including not being able to finish my books (now, in less than two years, I have written and published 30 best-sellers. My self-published book, 'Mid-Life Career Rescue' was an Amazon.com 2015 #1 bestseller. You'll find many of my other self-empowerment books here —Author.to/CassandraGaisford

Coaching Cassandra's Way Works! It Has Worked For Me and It Has Worked For My Clients

'Thank YOU! Our coaching was immensely helpful, and I have renewed hope for finding my way. You are simply lovely, and brilliant, and wise. So glad our energies aligned and I found you!'

~ Lisa Webb, artist, New York

"Cassandra has been great to work with. She's flexible in her approach, but also keeps the coaching sessions focused and productive. I was unsure about having the coaching via Skype, but it hasn't been a problem at all. I still feel a strong sense of immediacy and connection and come away from our sessions feeling energised and empowered."

~ **Jan, communications professional, New Zealand**

"A coaching session with Cassandra is like a light switch to a light bulb. My ideas were there but without that light switch, I wasn't able to see them and manifest my dream of running a holistic business from home. Straight away, Cassandra was able to get to the heart of my core values and how to put them into a dream business. I now have a sense of purpose and drive to achieve my business goals. Cassandra's warm personality and positive approach make her a joy to work with. I recommend her to anyone who wants to unlock their personal and professional potential."

~ **Shelley Sweeney, writer & Reiki practitioner, New Zealand**

Become the best version of yourself today

To schedule an appointment at a reduced fee of $100 NZD please navigate to here—http://www.cassandragaisford.com/schedule-an-appointment/

GAIN MORE HELP HERE

G ain unlimited lifetime access to my online courses, for as long as you like—across any and all devices you own. Be supported with practical, inspirational, easy-to-access strategies to achieve your dreams.

Follow your passion and purpose to prosperity

Easily discover your passion and purpose, overcoming barriers to success, and create a job or business you love.

To start achieving outstanding personal and professional results with absolute certainty and excitement. Click here to enrol or find out more>>https://the-coaching-lab.teachable. com/p/follow-your-passion-and-purpose-to-prosperity

5 Day Email Course: Career Rescue

How to confidently leave a job you hate, and start living a life you love: The Step by Step Guide to Changing Careers

>>https://the-coaching-lab.teachable.com/p/5-day-email-course-how-to-confidently-leave-a-job-you-hate-and-start-living-a-life-you-love

ONLY $33 USD

PLEASE LEAVE A REVIEW

Word of mouth is the most powerful marketing force in the universe. If you found this book useful, I'd appreciate you rating this book and leaving a review. You don't have to say much—just a few words about how the book helped you learn something new or made you feel.

"Your books are a fantastic resource and until now I never even thought to write a review. Going forward I will be reviewing more books. So many great ones out there and I want to support the amazing people that write them."

Great reviews help people find good books that change lives.

Thank you so much! I appreciate you!

PS: If you enjoyed this title or any of my books could you do me a huge favour and leave a review and help others by spreading the word about them and sharing links, or reviews on Facebook, Twitter, Instagram, and other social networks.

STAY IN TOUCH

Follow Me and Continue To Be Supported, Encouraged, and Inspired

www.cassandragaisford.com
www.facebook.com/cassandra.gaisford
www.instagram.com/cassandragaisford
www.youtube.com/cassandragaisfordnz
www.pinterest.com/cassandraNZ
www.linkedin.com/in/cassandragaisford
www.twitter.com/cassandraNZ

BLOG

Subscribe and be inspired by regular posts to help you increase your wellness, follow your bliss, slay self-doubt, and sustain healthy habits.

Learn more about how to achieve happiness and success at work and life by visiting my blog:

www.cassandragaisford.com/archives

SPEAKING EVENTS

Cassandra is available internationally for speaking events
aimed at wellness strategies, motivation, inspiration and as a
keynote speaker.

She has an enthusiastic, humorous and passionate style of
delivery and is celebrated for her ability to motivate, inspire
and enlighten.

For information navigate to www.cassandragaisford.com/
contact/speaking

To ask Cassandra to come and speak at your workplace or
conference, contact: cassandra@cassandragaisford.com

NEWSLETTERS

For inspiring tools and helpful tips subscribe to Cassandra's
free newsletters here:
http://www.cassandragaisford.com

**Sign up now and receive a free eBook to help you find
your passion and purpose!**

http://eepurl.com/bEArfT

COPYRIGHT

The intent of the author is only to offer information of a general nature to help you in your quest for emotional, physical, and spiritual well-being.

Any use of information in this book is at the reader's discretion and risk. Neither the author nor the publisher can be held responsible for any loss, claim or damage arising out of the use, or misuse, of the suggestions made, the failure to take medical advice or for any material on third party websites.

ISBN PRINT: 978-1-99-002057-5
ISBN EBOOK: 978-1-99-002056-8
ISBN HARDCOVER: 978-1-99-002058-2

First Edition

www.ingramcontent.com/pod-product-compliance
Lightning Source LLC
Chambersburg PA
CBHW031902200326
41597CB00012B/519